FOOTBALL TRICK SHORT GUY OF KASHMIR

STORY OF SHAH HUZAIB

IMRAN KASHMIRI

ruseruseru

GARAH WANDAI GARA SASAH, GARAH NERAHA NE ZAH

Translation: O Home, I offer you a thousand houses and I will never go out from you.

Meaning: There's no place like home.

ASAV NE, TE LASAV KITH PAETH

Translation: If we don't laugh, how will we live?

Meaning: He who laughs lives longer

HALEN BANAN VUKER THAAN, HIVEN HIVY SAMKHAAN

Translation: Twisted covers for twisted vessels.

Meaning: Like-minded persons meet like-minded persons (Birds with the same feathers flock together).

HASTI DAREYI NA WAVAH TIH BUJI KAED KAPAS

Translation: The elephants couldn't stand the wind, but the old woman went out.

Meaning: An insignificant person can often accomplish what kings have not.

KAHILO TSAENGIS DI PHOKH' ACH VATIV, TSONG GATSI TSHET PANAY

Translation: O lazy fellow, put off the lamp, close your eyes and the light will be extinguished.

Meaning: Laziness is a curse.

BOYI GOV KAEYN, BENI GAYIH THAIN

Translation and Meaning: The brother is hard like a stone, and the sister is soft like butter.

HOON WORAN THE KARWAN PAKAAN

Translation and Meaning: The dogs bark but the caravan goes on.

Contents

Foreword

❧ ❧ ❧

Amir Khusrau famously said " Gar firdaus bar rue zameen ast/hameen asto, hameen asto, hameen ast (If ever there is Paradise on Earth/It is here! It is here!

Challenges faced by Kashmir students :

Violence:- Due to constant fighting with the neighbouring country Pakistan something or the other is happening because of which there is shut down & curfew which prevent students from going to their respective school & college.

ARTICLE 370:- Converting Jammu & Kashmir as one of our Union Territories gave a due advantage to people living in Kashmir but not good for students as a complete lockdown and communications blockade (NO INTERNET, NO PHONE CALLS) was imposed on the Valley. Schools were not allowed to open & experience low or no attendance as parents were afraid to send their children to school.

Unemployment:- As students are unable to get a continuous flow of education thus they are unable to complete their course and result in unemployment because of lack of education.

Mental health:- According to a Doctor Without Borders study in 2016, 45%of the population in Kashmir experiencing "mental distress." From a child to an old age group, no one is safe from outside violence, no schooling leads to automatic mental stress.

Salary: Now the salary received by teachers is not enough to bear all the expenses of their families. They have to get on credits to meet their family demands. Even their kids are unable to enrol in school or colleges.

Online Learning:- In online learning there are various problem some of them are listed below:-

Internet speed:- The internet speed offered in Kashmir is 2G irrespective of all the video conferencing apps needing a basic 4Ginternet speed to operate because of which either due to connection error unable to hear the voice or leave the meeting.

2. *Examination:- There are many children unable to give exams because of a lack of learning and others giving exams either by copying it from Google or a textbook.*

.No interaction:- If somehow students join the meeting they are unable to see their respective teachers they can maximum show the movement of hands as they start receiving threat calls.

4. Missing going to school:- Apart from Jammu & Kashmir students, the rest of the country's students have been saying this since March 2020 but Kashmir students are facing this issue for more than 11years.

There are other challenges as well such as in rural areas of Kashmir the females are not allowed to get an education, for them now online is also not possible thus the literacy rate of Kashmir is very low as compared to other states of India.

Preface

❧❧❧

B. Initiatives:

Aawo Padhain:-The Directorate of School Education Kashmir has set up "Aawo Padhain" which means Come Let's Study. It is an e-portal that is filled with e-content of video-base classes, and a free child helpline that provides aid and assistance to children.

C. Recommendation

Planning the Proper Location of Schools – Schools should be available to the student in 1km, 3kms, 5kms, and 7kms radii respectively.

Institutional Planning – At the time of curfew how schools and colleges are going to continue with their teaching which type of strategy should be adopted?

General Education and Training of Teachers should be made compulsory

Qualitative Upgrading of Schools For successful educational transformation & To bridge the overall gap in education in Kashmir needs well-qualified teachers, access to electricity, the internet, computers, technology, and libraries.

Supervision – The overall check on administration, enrollment, teaching and other departments such be done regularly to improve their children's productivity.

Improvement In Textbooks and Methods of Teaching as per the need should be evaluated.

Acknowledgements

Born:- 2002 (age 20–21)

Resident:- Charari Sharief, Jammu and Kashmir (state), India

Nationality:- Indian

Known for:-football trick-shots

Awards:-Kashmiri Young Achievers' Award 2021

Prologue

Shah Huzaib is a freestyle footballer from the Budgam district of Jammu and Kashmir known for his trick shots. He attracted news headlines after former Indian footballer Bhaichung Bhutia, Bollywood actor Sunil Shetty and German soccer player Toni Kroos shared his videos on Instagram.

Born in 2002, Shah Huzaib hails from Charari Sharief in the Budgam district. In 2016, he started playing football, and in May 2018, he started practicing football trick shots. After his videos became viral on social media, he became one of the most famous football trick-shot artists. In 2020, Huzaib participated in and won an international football trick-shot competition, which has been organized by Cristiano Ronaldo Fragrances.

In 2021, Huzaib attracted various news headlines when former Indian footballer Bhaichung Bhutia and Bollywood actor Sunil Shetty praised him on social media.

As of 2021, Huzaib has recorded more than 400 trick shots. He learned trick shots from YouTube. He looks up to footballer Cristiano Ronaldo as an inspiration.

In January 2022, German soccer player Toni Kroos also shared Huzaib's trick-shots video.

He has been invited to several television shows including India's Got Talent Season 9.

In football, trick shots basically involve scoring goals by overcoming obstacles and in various styles. It's rare to see footballers engaging in trick shots in India, and even rarer in Kashmir. But Shah Huzaib, a teenager from central Kashmir's Budgam district, has stunned people with his skills. Shah (18) can kick a football from a long distance and through moving tires and baskets. His shots can also knock off small bottles placed on the heads of people, and trick shots of this nature have made this teenager a social media star. After two years of practicing rigorously, Shah finally started doing trick shots in 2018. "To do trick shots, you need to know the game very well. So I learned football first. My family always appreciates my endeavors and it is a constant support system for me," says Shah, with a smile.

The videos of his trick shots have also been featured on social media sites including 'Oh My Goal' and 'People Are Awesome' which have a huge following across the globe. One of his videos titled 'Insane trick-shot — in which he kicked a tennis ball through two moving tape rolls — generated around five million views on 'People are Awesome'. With thousands of followers on his various social media accounts, Huzaib performs scores of trick shots using balls of all sizes. Discovering trick shots During the political unrest triggered after the killing of Hizbul Mujahideen militant commander Burhan

Wani in July 2016, Shah, then a 13-year-old boy, remained confined inside his home. "However, to kill boredom, I started playing football on my lawn all alone. Since the game requires a team to play, I found a strange way by trying to learn football tricks," he tells. He kept playing the traditional form of football until he stumbled over some football trick-shot videos on YouTube. "I was amazed at what one of the guys did. I felt captivated by his gravity-defying tricks. I tried to emulate some of the tricks on my lawn. I fell in love with what he did. I wanted to do the same," he explains. Shah adds, "I started practicing tricks for hours in the morning and evening before I slowly started getting better at it." Possessing an incredible talent for hand-eye coordination, Shah would often perform tricks without looking at the target, which would be behind him.

He does not let his passion for trick shots affect his academics at all. After scoring distinction in Class X, Huzaib opted to study science for higher studies. The trickster wants to continue his education so that he can combine his love for 'science and art' with trick shots. Shah now wants to be a star footballer and his favorites on the field are Cristiano Ronaldo, David Beckham, and Isco Alarcon. "On my list of top trick-shot stars are Jed Hockin, Liam Coyte, and Matanos, all from Europe. I want more trick shot stars to emerge from the valley so that this game gets recognition here."

Shah pointed out that no government has supported him so far. "I have not received any help from the government so far. Some of the officials only write on social media about helping any talent but no one had come forward to provide help. These people have power and can do anything," he explains He urged the government to provide him with all the facilities so that he can reach the national or international level. "Give me facilities so that I can pass my skills to the youth of our Valley. All those who play football can also understand and learn and play trick shots,"

Kashmir Young Achievers Award 2021

www.ingramcontent.com/pod-product-compliance
Lightning Source LLC
Chambersburg PA
CBHW030512170726
47990CB00008BA/3176